GEOGRAPHY FACT FILES

POLAR REGIONS

Paul Mason

HODDER
Wayland

an imprint of Hodder Children's Books

GEOGRAPHY FACT FILES

Produced by Monkey Puzzle Media Ltd

Gissing's Farm, Fressingfield, Suffolk IP21 5SH, UK

First published in 2004 by Hodder Wayland

An imprint of Hodder Children's Books

Text copyright © 2004 Hodder Wayland

Volume copyright © 2004 Hodder Wayland

Editor   Nicola Edwards

Designer   Jamie Asher

Picture Researcher   Sally Cole

Illustrator   Michael Posen

Consultant   Michael Allaby

Printed in China

Cover: The Tracy Arm fjord, Alaska

Title page picture: Adult emperor penguins shelter their chicks from a blizzard in Antarctica.

British Library Cataloguing in Publication Data

Mason, Paul, 1967–

  Polar regions. – (Geography fact files)

  1.Human ecology – Polar regions – Juvenile literature

  2.Polar regions – Juvenile literature

  I.Title

  919.8

ISBN 07502 4401 1

Acknowledgements

We are grateful to the following for permission to reproduce photographs: Alamy 35 top (Brian Atkinson); Bryan and Cherry Alexander *back cover left*, 1 (Steve Pinfield), 3 top and middle, 4, 6, 9 top, 10 both, 11 (Steve Pinfield), 13 bottom, 14, 15, 16 (Steve Pinfield), 17, 18, 19, 21, 26, 27 top, 28, 29, 31 top, 36, 37, 42, 44; Corbis 25 bottom (Bettmann), 38 (Natalie Fobes), 39 (Caroline Penn); Getty Images *front cover* (Art Wolfe); Mary Evans Picture Library 23; Nature Picture Library 3 bottom (Martha Holmes), 33 (Martha Holmes), 34 (Mike Salisbury), 43 bottom (Staffan Widstrand); Old Dartmouth Historical Society, New Bedford Whaling Museum 20; Popperfoto.com 24, 25 top; Science Photo Library 30 (British Antarctic Survey); Still Pictures 8 (Anne Piantanida), 12 (Klein/Hubert), 13 top (Juan Carlos Munoz), 32 (J J Alcalay), 35 bottom (Gunter Ziesler), 41 (Anne Piantanida), 43 top (Hartmut Schwarzbach), 45 (Emmanuel Jeanjean); Werner Forman Archive 22 (The Greenland Museum).

Hodder Childen's Books

A division of Hodder Headline Limited

338 Euston Road, London NW1 3BH

CONTENTS

The words that are explained in the glossary are printed in **bold** the first time they are mentioned in the text.

WHAT ARE POLAR REGIONS?

1magine a land so cold that few living creatures can survive. It has no visible plants, animals or human inhabitants. All that's there is a desert-like expanse of snow and ice, with perhaps a few rocky outcrops. The lands you're imagining exist, at the heart of the world's polar regions.

SIMILARITIES AND DIFFERENCES

The polar regions lie around the North and South Poles. They share common characteristics, most obviously a harsh, freezing-cold climate that makes living at the poles themselves almost impossible (though a scientific research station is kept at the South Pole). But there are also important differences between the northern and southern polar regions.

Deep beneath the ice of the South Pole is a landmass, the continent of Antarctica. Antarctica expands and contracts its area depending on the time of year: the shelf of ice around its coast shrinks in summer and grows bigger during winter. But at all times Antarctica is surrounded by the barrier of the Southern Ocean.

A fishing settlement in Newfoundland, Canada.

The Arctic region is defined in different ways: by latitude (the Arctic Circle), temperature (the 50 °F isotherm) and vegetation (the treeline).

The North Pole and the Arctic regions that surround it are sited on the thick ice of the Arctic Ocean. No landmass lies beneath the ice. Instead, the Arctic is surrounded by the northern edges of three continents: North America, Europe and Asia. People from these continents have lived on the fringes of the Arctic for centuries.

50 °F (10 °C) isotherm

Treeline

Alaska

Canada

Russia

North Geographic Pole

Greenland

Arctic Circle

Europe

FACT FILE

THE FIVE NORTH POLES
There is more than one North Pole! (In this book 'North Pole' refers to the north geographic pole.)
• THE NORTH GEOGRAPHIC POLE lies near the centre of the Arctic Ocean, where all the Earth's lines of longitude meet.
• THE INSTANTANEOUS NORTH POLE lies at the point where the Earth's axis meets the surface. The Earth wobbles slowly as it turns around its axis, so the instantaneous pole moves. It travels clockwise around an irregular path called the Chandler Circle.
• THE NORTH POLE OF BALANCE lies at the centre of the Chandler Circle. Its position locates the north geographic pole. Each year since 1900, the north pole of balance has moved about 15 cm towards North America.
• THE NORTH MAGNETIC POLE is the farthest point on the Earth in the direction of magnetic north. This pole can move many kilometres in a few years.
• THE GEOMAGNETIC NORTH POLE lies in Greenland. In the Earth's upper atmosphere, the magnetic field points towards this point.

DEFINING POLAR REGIONS
The edges of the areas we call 'polar regions' can be defined in several ways. One is to use a map, which shows both the Arctic and Antarctic Circle. These lie 66 degrees and 30 minutes north and south of the Equator, and about 2,613 km from the respective poles. The circles mark the furthest point at which the Sun theoretically stays in the sky for 24 hours at midsummer, and doesn't rise at all for 24 hours at midwinter.

Another way of defining polar regions is based on climate. In the Arctic, for example, scientists have recorded the point at which the average summer temperature is 50 °F (10 °C). This line is known as the 50 °F isotherm, and can be used to mark the edge of the polar lands.

The 50 °F isotherm coincides with another defining point for Arctic lands: the treeline. This is the northernmost point at which trees can grow; further north, the short growing season and freezing temperatures mean trees cannot survive.

THE ARCTIC

nlike the South Pole, which is above land, the North Pole lies over the sea. A thick, permanent layer of ice known as the polar ice cap separates any explorer standing at the Pole from the ocean. This ice cap changes its size, growing larger in winter as more ice freezes in the cold temperatures, then shrinking in summer as higher temperatures lead to a thaw.

ISLANDS AND CONTINENTS

In places the ice cap touches on the lands that surround the Arctic Ocean (see map on page 5). Northern parts of the USA, Canada, Norway, Sweden, Finland and Russia all have territories that fringe the Arctic. There are also several groups of islands in the region, especially around the top of North America.

FACT FILE

THE ARCTIC OCEAN

The Arctic Ocean is the smallest of the world's five oceans (after the Pacific, Atlantic, Indian and Southern oceans).

• LOCATION The body of water between Europe, Asia and North America, mostly north of the Arctic Circle

• AREA Total: 14.056 million km²

• COASTLINE 45,389 km

• LOWEST POINT Fram Basin –4,665 m (highest point: sea level 0 m)

• NATURAL RESOURCES Sand and gravel aggregates, mineral deposits, polymetallic nodules, oil and gas fields, fish, marine mammals (seals and whales)

• ENVIRONMENTAL ISSUES Endangered marine species include walruses and whales; the fragile ecosystem is slow to change and slow to recover from disruptions or damage; the polar pack ice is thinning.

A Russian nuclear-powered icebreaker carves a path through thick sea ice in the Arctic Ocean.

In addition, other countries touch on the **sub-Arctic**. The sub-Arctic is almost as cold as the Arctic in the winter, but has warmer summers that allow a short growing season for plants. These sub-Arctic areas are usually thought by geographers to be part of the Arctic.

EXTENT OF THE ICE

During winter, pack ice covers almost the entire Arctic Ocean. This is frozen sea water, which becomes icy at –2 °C. By March, only the coasts of Norway and Russia as far as the White Sea are free of pack ice. Most pack ice is less than 2 m thick, and sometimes **icebreakers** are able to plough a way through it.

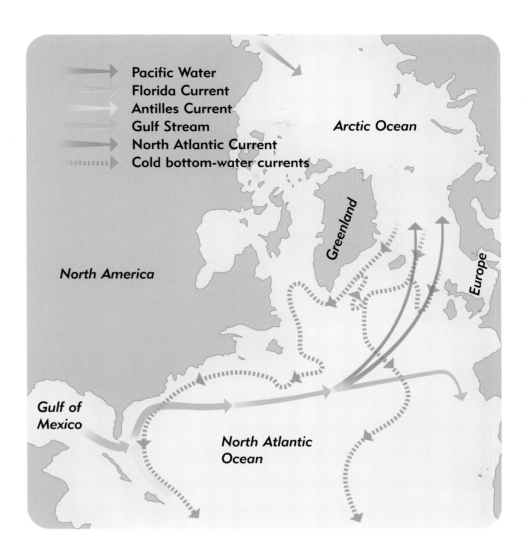

Pacific Water
Florida Current
Antilles Current
Gulf Stream
North Atlantic Current
Cold bottom-water currents

Arctic Ocean

Greenland

Europe

North America

Gulf of Mexico

North Atlantic Ocean

This map shows ocean currents in the Arctic and North Atlantic oceans. Cold bottom water flowing out of the Arctic is one of the world's most important ocean currents.

LOCATION FILE

THE BERING STRAIT
Named after the Danish navigator who first explored these northern waters, the Bering Strait is a short stretch of water separating North America from Asia.

During the **Cold War** the Bering Strait became one of the most heavily defended frontiers in the world. The USA and the **USSR** set up military installations and listening posts in an effort to spy on one another and prevent an invasion from the north.

ARCTIC OCEAN CURRENTS

The Arctic's ocean currents have an important effect on the climate of nearby regions. For example, the warm current known as the Gulf Stream is powered partly by a cycle of cold, salty water sinking to the bottom. This is then replaced at the surface by warmer water flowing from the Gulf of Mexico. This warm water gives regions such as north-west Scotland a warmer climate than they would otherwise experience. In the meantime, cold Arctic bottom water flows south towards the Antarctic in a powerful current that helps power the movement of ocean waters.

THE ANTARCTIC

U nlike in the Arctic, hidden below the Antarctic ice cap is an actual landmass. Without its ice this would be the smallest of the world's seven continents. Including the ice cap, however, the Antarctic covers about 14 million km² and is larger than either Europe or Australia.

THE ANTARCTIC ICE CAP

The Antarctic ice cap is an average of roughly 2,200 m thick. This means that Antarctica is the highest continent in terms of average elevation, at 2,300 m above sea level. Peeking up through the ice cap in places are Antarctica's mountains: the Antarctic Peninsula, pointing up towards Cape Horn; the Trans Antarctic Mountains; and several other, minor ranges.

Some of the ice at the Antarctic's edge has slowly been pushed there from much further inland, and is thousands of years old.

AN ANCIENT, ICY WORLD

Less than 1 per cent of Antarctica is free of ice and snow, and the region contains 90 per cent of the world's total amount of ice. If all this water melted, the oceans would rise by about 60–65 m. During winter, the sea ice that surrounds Antarctica more than doubles the continent's area.

In places Antarctica's ice is so old that scientists are able to discover information about the climate of the Earth thousands of years ago, by examining the atmospheric traces left behind. They have been able to peer through this icy window on the past and see back 400,000 years (see page 41).

Seeming as though it goes on forever, this is the Ekstrom Ice Shelf beside the Weddell Sea in Antarctica. Despite the sunshine, new ice is forming on the ocean.

FACT FILE

THE ANTARCTIC
* NAME Antarctica
* AREA 14.25 million km²
* POPULATION Around 1,200 excluding tourists
* GOVERNMENT No country governs Antarctica; it is administered by the Antarctic Treaty (see page 37). A number of countries claim territorial rights or maintain bases in Antarctica. They include:

From Europe: France, Britain, Poland, Germany, Ukraine and Russia

From Asia and Australasia: Australia, New Zealand, South Korea, India and Japan

From North and South America: Chile, Argentina, USA, Brazil and Uruguay

From Africa: South Africa.

This means that countries from each of the world's other six continents could one day claim a slice of the seventh.

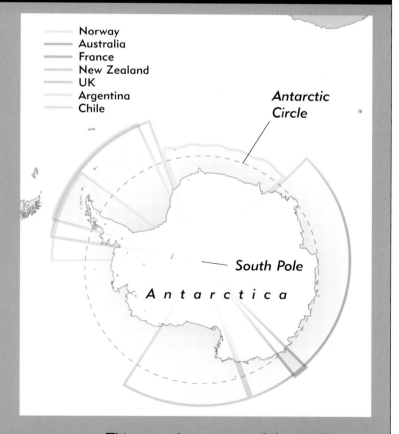

Norway
Australia
France
New Zealand
UK
Argentina
Chile

Antarctic Circle

South Pole

Antarctica

This map shows some of the overlapping claims to Antarctic territory.

A WORLD OF ICE

The features of the polar landscape are unlike anywhere else on Earth. Even though the polar regions contain almost all the world's **fresh water**, it is frozen solid. So little **precipitation** falls in the interior of the Antarctic that it can be classed as a desert. This dry landscape offers little chance of survival for plants, so even where the ground is exposed nothing grows.

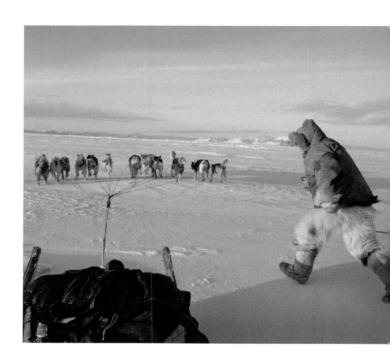

An Inuit hunter races to catch his dog sled. The Inuit successfully adapted to life in the Arctic when they arrived there over 1000 years ago.

FACT FILE

Above **Icebergs form when part of an ice shelf like this one breaks away. The biggest can be the size of a medium-sized island, even though most of the iceberg is underwater.**

ICEBERGS

• From 80 to 90 per cent of most icebergs is underwater. But as little as 50 per cent and as much as 99 per cent can be underwater, depending on the amount of air trapped inside.

• Pieces of ice that lie mainly or entirely underwater are known as 'growlers'.

• Icebergs are made of fresh water, not sea water.

• One of the biggest icebergs ever seen broke free from the Ross Ice Shelf in Antarctica in 1995. Above water it was 295 km long and 37 km wide – about the size of Connecticut in the United States. Below the surface it was ten times as big.

THE VINSON MASSIF

The Vinson Massif (above) is the highest point on Antarctica. This means it is on the 'tick list' (meaning things to do) of those who want to have climbed the highest peak on each of the seven continents. This has lead to one of the more curious industries in Antarctica – mountain guiding, where specialist climbers escort those with less experience to the top.

Above **The peak of Mount Vinson, which has now been reached by an increasing number of climbers who are wealthy enough to join an expedition there.**

COMPACTED SNOW

When snow first falls it is very light, and has a **density** roughly one-third that of solid ice. However, as more snow falls on top of it, the layer underneath begins to be crushed down. Slowly, over decades, it is compacted until it becomes solid ice. This is how the permanent ice cap built up around the South Pole, from snow blown there from the coast by Antarctica's fierce winds.

In the Antarctic, there is a limit to how thick the ice cap can become. Too much pressure from above causes the ice to flow slowly outwards, a millimetre at a time. It flows over or around obstacles to the sea. In some places under the surface the ice is warmer than where it is exposed, and it can even melt, creating ice streams which help lubricate the ice's progress towards the sea.

ICEBERGS AND SEA ICE

When the ice cap meets the sea, it spreads out over the surface of the water for a long way. However, sometimes, huge chunks of ice break away and float off. These are icebergs. Usually they are held fast in sea ice during the winter, but in summer when the sea ice melts giant icebergs are sometimes released that can become a hazard to shipping.

TUNDRA AND TAIGA

On the fringes of the Arctic are two zones that surround the northern polar region. They are known as the tundra and taiga. Typically they have winters that are almost as cold as those of the Arctic itself, but the summers are warmer, allowing a growing season for plants and, in the taiga, trees. The Antarctic's thick ice cannot support tundra or taiga.

THE TUNDRA

Tundra is the name given to the treeless plains that surround the Arctic. The ground thaws in the summer, allowing low-growing plants to put down roots. These include mosses, lichens, grasses and shrubs. **Migratory** birds and other animals spread into the region, enjoying the brief flush of life summer brings. Others, like the Arctic fox, emerge from their winter coats and adopt a different camouflage from the white they have been wearing during the snowy times. **Meltwater** forms ponds, small lakes and swamps, which freeze again in winter. Usually only the top 30–300 cm of soil thaws; below that the ground is always frozen. This is called **permafrost**.

The Arctic fox is able to change its coat from winter white to summer colours, which will blend in better with the tundra landscape.

THE TAIGA

South of the tundra lies a zone where the soil thaws more deeply. Here trees such as dwarf willows, birches and alders grow. They rarely manage to reach heights of more than 12 m, because their roots cannot grow to support a greater height than this. Reindeer moss – so-called because it is eaten by reindeer – covers large areas of ground in a thick, spongy carpet. Further south again is the taiga: great forests of trees such as cedars, firs, pines, spruce and birch.

The border between the taiga forests of the Denali National Park in Alaska, USA, and the tundra that lies further north.

This has become a major resource for loggers. Although the winter lasts for seven or eight months, the growing season has long hours of daylight in which plants can **photosynthesize**. There is also reliable rainfall, so a lot of growth can be packed into a short summer.

LOCATION FILE

THULE, GREENLAND

One major tundra region is Thule in north-west Greenland. Lying about 10° north of the Arctic Circle, Thule is the site of a US airbase, so it provides many Americans with their first experience of Arctic living. It is named after 'Ultima Thule' a place described roughly 2000 years ago by a Greek writer named Pytheas. 'Ultima Thule' was the most northern land known – Pytheas said that the days and nights lasted six months each, and the ice was so thick it could not be rowed through.

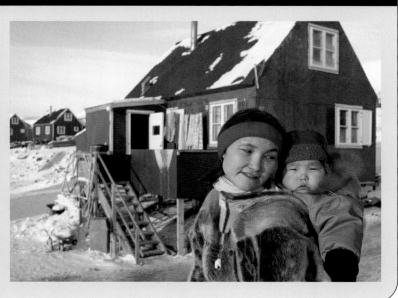

CLIMATE

The climate of the polar regions varies depending on how near to the pole you are. But all regions would seem extremely cold during winter to anyone who had never visited them before. They are also extremely dry: the Antarctic interior gets so little rain that it is technically a desert, and the Arctic is also a parched land.

EXTREMES OF COLD

Most household freezers run at about –20 °C. In the Arctic, the average winter temperature is about –34 °C. The coldest weather of all is found in north-eastern Siberia, where the January average is –40 °C, and a lowest-ever temperature of –69 °C has been recorded. Temperatures in Antarctica regularly fall even lower.

FACT FILE

HIGHS AND LOWS

LOCATION	MONTH	TEMP. (°C)
Faraday Station, Antarctica	December	0
	August	–10
South Pole	December	–28
	August	–60
Vostock Station, Antarctica	December	–32
	August	–67

This hunter from Igloolik, in Canada's North-west Territories, is out in the sunshine of a –40 °C day. No wonder his breath has frozen solid on his moustache and eyebrows and his caribou-skin hood.

Nearer to the coast, both polar regions have warmer climates. In the Antarctic summertime, January inland temperatures only reach about –15 °C. At the coasts they may reach 0 °C. Some northern islands even manage 10 °C – not exactly sunbathing weather, but not so cold that your hand would freeze to any metal it touches, as it would in winter!

The Arctic climate also changes depending on how near to the sea you are. Average summer temperatures near the Atlantic and Pacific Oceans are 7 °C. However, inland parts of Siberia and North America are even warmer in summer, with highs of 32 °C or more.

DRY REGIONS

Rainfall in the Arctic averages about 15–25 cm a year, including melted snow. If this seems low, compared with the Antarctic it's a lot. The interior **plateau** of Antarctica averages just 5 cm of snow a year (less than 50 mm of water). Even on the coast an average of just 60 cm of snow falls. The average at the South Pole itself is about 25 mm of rainfall equivalent.

It's important to wear plenty of layers of clothes, even when you're busy playing. Air trapped between the layers warms up, keeping you warmer than a single layer might.

LOCATION FILE

THE COLDEST PLACE ON EARTH

• The coldest average temperature was recorded at Plateau Station, Antarctica, with an average of –56.6 °C.
• The coldest temperature ever recorded was at Vostok Station, Antarctica. The temperature gauge there fell to -89.2 °C, on 21 July 1983.

WEATHER

The polar regions experience some of the most violent weather conditions on Earth. Extremely powerful winds batter the landscape, especially in winter. In coastal regions, especially in the sub-Arctic, heavy snow can trap people indoors for days on end. Parts of the Arctic even suffer from extreme heat – in the middle of summer, the temperature can rise above 32 °C!

POLAR WINDS

Both polar regions experience very high wind speeds. These add a **wind chill** factor to the temperature, whereby the force of the wind takes heat away from living things more quickly than if there were no wind. In the Antarctic winter, **katabatic winds** flow down from the interior towards the coast as cold air is drawn to the warmer regions near the ocean.

Adult emperor penguins have surrounded a group of their chicks as a way of offering them some shelter from a blizzard.

FACT FILE

A WEIGHT OF ICE

• Antarctica is pushed into the Earth by the weight of the ice that covers it. If all the ice were removed, the continent would spring up by about 500 m – but very slowly. It would grow an average of about 5 cm a year.

• Scotland and Scandinavia, also buried under an ice sheet at one time, are both still rebounding. The 'fastest' place is in the northern Baltic – where the growth is about 5 mm a year.

A sudden winter storm hits the community of Savissivick in north-west Greenland.

STORMS

In the Arctic winter, storms develop mainly in two areas where the air temperature is almost always low. The first is the Aleutian low, which extends from eastern Siberia to the Gulf of Alaska. The second is the Icelandic low, which covers central Canada, the Arctic Ocean, and part of the northern Atlantic and northern Europe. Weather stations in Alaska warn of storms approaching northern North America, while forecasters in Greenland and Iceland help to predict storms arriving in Europe.

To the north of the Antarctic lies a belt of strong westerly winds. These drive both weather and the ocean currents, at a latitude known as the 'Roaring Forties'. Ocean-racing yachts often try to use the Roaring Forties to gain speed. But these are dangerous waters, and many sailors have lost their lives here through the years.

Occasionally storm systems develop in the Roaring Forties and spin down towards Antarctica. They bring strong winds and heavy snow to the coasts, but few ever reach the high interior plateau.

 ## LOCATION FILE

CAPE DENISON, ADÉLIE LAND COAST, ANTARCTICA
• On the steep coastal slopes of Cape Denison, the Antarctic's katabatic winds accelerate to very high speeds of over 700 kph.
• In 1912-13 an expedition led by Sir Douglas Mawson recorded a world-record sustained wind speed of 19.4 m per second.
• On all but one of 203 days during winter the expedition experienced gale-force winds.

POLAR OCEANS

Most scientists place the northern limit of the Antarctic Ocean between 40° and 60° south latitude, though its boundaries are not universally agreed. The Arctic Ocean is usually said to be made up of most of the waters that lie north of the Arctic Circle. Groups of islands divide the ocean into seven seas (see fact file on page 19).

FROZEN SURFACES

During winter, large areas of both polar oceans are frozen over. About 70 per cent of the Arctic Ocean is covered in ice throughout the year. This ice circulates slowly in a clockwise direction, driven by the easterly airflow of the region and its ocean currents. The Antarctic Ocean develops ice along the coastline of Antarctica. In summer the ice occupies over 2.5 million km²; in winter, it can spread to more than 20.5 million km².

Very few Arctic ports stay open all year round, because sea ice freezes so hard and deep that ships cannot escape. They have to sit ice-bound in the harbour, waiting for the spring thaw.

LOCATION FILE

DRAKE PASSAGE

The Antarctic Ocean's narrowest point is the 1000-km gap between Antarctica and Tierra del Fuego, the southern tip of South America. Here, wind-driven currents push 140,000,000 m³ of water a second through the Drake Passage. This is roughly 5,000 times the flow of the Amazon River.

OCEAN CURRENTS

Near to Antarctica, the winds flow in an easterly direction, causing the ocean current around the continent to flow east as well. Further north, strong westerly winds create a west-flowing current. The place where these two currents rub against one another is known as the Antarctic Divergence. Further north still, the Antarctic Convergence marks the place where warmer waters meet the cold polar sea.

Over half the water that flows into the Arctic Ocean comes from the North Atlantic Current, flowing between Iceland and Norway. Most of the rest flows north from the Pacific, through the Bering Strait. Water leaves the ocean in the East Greenland Current and through a current that flows through the islands of the Canadian Arctic. Bottom-water moving south from the Arctic is known as the Great Conveyor, which finally joins the Circumpolar Current in the Antarctic.

RESOURCES

A lthough they appear to be barren lands covered by snow for much of each year, the polar regions are rich in resources. Whether these should be exploited is a constant source of conflict. The Antarctic is protected by an international treaty that prevents any commercial activity. The Arctic has no treaty, and its resources have been plundered by people from the south for hundreds of years.

WHALE HO!

One of the first Arctic resources to be exploited was whales. In the 1600s whaling became a major industry in Europe, and demand for **whale oil**, **spermaceti** and **baleen** became unquenchable. Whale products were used for lamp oil at a time when lamps were almost the only source of light, as well as in clothing manufacture and many other processes. By the 1700s whalers had spread their activities throughout the Arctic. It was the crew of a whaling ship that first set foot on the continent of Antarctica. So many whales were killed that in the early 1700s the US whaling fleet alone was taking about 10,000 a year. Their numbers dropped so low that today whales are protected, and may only be hunted for scientific purposes.

The whaling ship *Essex* being attacked and sunk by a giant male sperm whale, an incident that inspired the novel *Moby Dick*. Whales rarely came out of encounters with whaling ships on the winning side, however, and hundreds of thousands were hunted during the nineteenth and twentieth centuries.

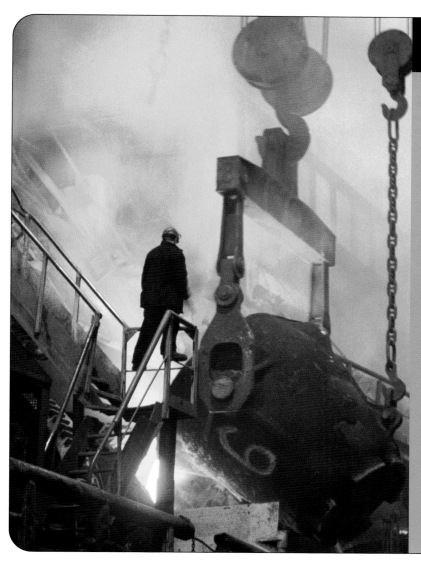

MINERAL RESOURCES

Though both polar areas have mineral deposits, the Antarctic's seem unlikely to be profitable to extract.

• The Arctic's mineral resources include: coal, radioactive minerals such as thorium and uranium, iron, lead, nickel, gold, cryolite, copper and tin.

• The Antarctic's mineral deposits include: copper, chromium, gold, iron, lead, molybendum, zinc and coal.

Left **This man is working at a copper foundry in Siberia. Copper-rich rocks are turned into useful metal, which can be transported further south for use by industry.**

FISHING

Some of the world's richest fishing grounds lie along the edges of polar regions, off the coasts of Greenland and Iceland. In the Antarctic, the seas are rich in krill, small shrimp-like creatures which in large numbers can turn the ocean red by their colour. The krill attract many kinds of fish, which in turn attract fishing vessels to the region's seas.

WEALTH UNDER THE GROUND

The Antarctic continent has various minerals, including gold. These minerals occur in small amounts, and because of the difficult climate it would probably not be worthwhile to extract them.

The lands that fringe the Arctic Ocean are home to a variety of minerals, most of which are worth mining. Oil and natural gas are also found in valuable quantities. Greenland is the site of the world's only large deposit of cryolite, which is used in making aluminium and glass.

FORESTS

The trees of the taiga can reach up to 25 m in height. The forests that fringe the polar lands have been logged for centuries, but in the last 100 years they have begun to disappear at a far higher rate than ever before. In parts of eastern North America, for example, less than two per cent of the original forest cover remains.

EARLY HISTORY

Thousands of years ago people in search of new lands began to use a land bridge formed by the dry Bering Strait (which has now disappeared beneath the ocean) to cross from Asia to North America. These early travellers were just passing through the polar regions, however. It was only the last group of emigrants from Asia who stayed put in the Arctic. Today their descendants are known as the Inuit, Aleut and Yuit peoples.

LIVING AS A GROUP

Life in the harsh conditions of the Arctic was extremely tough. Everyone was expected to help with the day-to-day activities that made life possible. Behaviour that threatened the group could result in **banishment**. Since individuals cannot survive alone in the Arctic, banishment was nearly always a death sentence.

When food was plentiful Inuit people lived in groups that could include several hundred members. For example, during spring and autumn in Alaska the caribou migrated, and large groups gathered at the best hunting grounds. When food was less plentiful people split into smaller groups that would find it easier to feed themselves.

FOOD AND CLOTHING

With few plants available to eat, people had to survive mainly by hunting. Most groups lived near the sea, where they caught whales and seals, as well as Arctic char, salmon and other fish. On land they hunted caribou, as well as smaller animals like hares and foxes.

The Inuit dressed in clothes made of animal skins: caribou was considered best (as the animal was easiest to catch and its large hide was both warm and hard-wearing), followed by sealskin, fox, polar bear and other skins. People wore a hooded jacket called a *parka*, trousers, boots and mittens, as well as other layers on the inside for warmth.

The 500-year-old face of a mummified Inuit child, found with seven other mummies in Greenland in 1972.

When this photo was taken in 1910, the way of life of northern people had begun to change. Even so, these women could not have imagined that their grandchildren would one day be using snowmobiles to get around.

TRANSPORT AND SHELTER

During the summer, most people walked on land and travelled by boat on water. They spent most of their time living in tents.

In winter, people travelled the ice using dog sleds. For shelter, they dug down into the ground, then lined the hole with stones. Wood or whalebone made the roof, which was covered in earth. Often the entrance to this kind of house was underground, so that the warm air inside could not rise into the outside air and escape.

 FACT FILE

ANIMAL USES

Arctic peoples used every possible part of the animals they caught. Some of the uses they found for parts of the animals are quite surprising:

• People often wore goggles to protect their eyes from the glare of the Sun on the snow. These could be made of bone or **walrus ivory**, and covered the eyes. They had small holes or slits to look through.

• Seal or caribou skins were used to cover the tents people usually lived in during summer.

• **Kayaks** and **umiaks** (both a kind of boat) were made of wooden frameworks covered in sealskin.

POLAR EXPLORATION

Explorers who aimed to reach the actual sites of the North and South Poles had to be able to deal with the extreme cold, high winds and snowstorms that are common in the polar regions. The North Pole, more accessible from inhabited areas, was reached first, in 1909. Then in 1911 the South Pole was reached.

EARLY ARCTIC EXPLORERS

The first people to explore the Arctic regions were migrants from Asia, who we now know as the Inuit, Aleut and Yuit people (see pages 22–23). The first Europeans interested in Arctic exploration were looking for a way to reach Asia by travelling through the icy northern seas. This dreamed-of route was known as the **North-west Passage**, and many men died trying to discover if it really existed.

FACT FILE

POLAR MILESTONES
- 1570s Martin Frobisher journeys into Arctic regions searching for the North-west Passage.
- 1773 James Cook crosses the Antarctic Circle while searching for Antarctica.
- 1820 Antarctica is seen for the first time.
- 1839–43 James Ross is the first to journey beyond the pack ice surrounding Antarctica.
- 1845 Sir John Franklin's expedition disappears while searching for a sea route around northern North America.
- 1901–02 Robert Scott leads the first inland exploration of Antarctica.
- 1909 Robert Peary reaches the North Pole.
- 1911 Roald Amundsen reaches the South Pole.

THE NORTH POLE IS REACHED

In the late 1800s explorers began to visit the Arctic hoping to become the first to reach the Pole. Robert E Peary of the USA is said to have led the expedition that got there first, on 6 April 1909. He travelled to the Pole with Matthew Henson and four Inuit men on dog sleds.

Admiral Robert E Peary of the USA, credited with leading the first successful expedition to the North Pole.

ANTARCTIC EXPLORATION

The first people to sight Antarctica almost certainly set eyes on it in 1820. Three sailors – British and Russian navy officers and an American sealer – separately reached points where the continent was visible. It wasn't until 1895 that a Norwegian named Henryk Johan Bull and his crew of whalers actually set foot on Antarctica.

RACE TO THE SOUTH POLE

By the early 1900s several explorers were aiming to be the first to journey to the South Pole. By 1911, it had become a race between two teams, led by Roald Amundsen of Norway and Robert Scott of Great Britain. Scott's expedition aimed to use ponies and motor sleds to drag equipment, but these became bogged down in the snow. The men were forced to drag much of their gear themselves.

Amundsen, by contrast, was using Inuit techniques to make better progress. He and his four assistants travelled by ski, reaching the Pole on 14 December 1911 and returning to their base camp safely. Scott reached the Pole on 17 January 1912. He and his team of four men died during the attempt to return home.

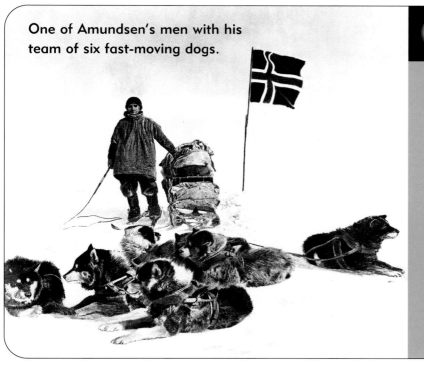

One of Amundsen's men with his team of six fast-moving dogs.

FACT FILE

LEARNING FROM THE INUIT

The expeditions that reached the Poles first made use of Inuit techniques for travel and survival:

• Dog teams hauled equipment, making faster progress than the men possibly could dragging the gear themselves.

• When killed and eaten, the dogs provided emergency food supplies.

• The explorers journeyed on skis, and wore relatively light, warm furs to survive the freezing temperatures.

POLAR PEOPLES

The biting cold and extreme weather of the actual Poles ought to mean that no one lives there. But in fact the USA has maintained an international scientific research base at the South Pole since 1956. No one lives at the North Pole, but native people and a few others do live near enough to be called inhabitants of the Arctic, rather than sub-Arctic.

ANTARCTIC RESEARCH STATIONS

The only people living on the Antarctic continent are those based at scientific research stations. The most amazing of these is the USA's Amundsen-Scott South Pole Station, which is actually at the Pole. But many other countries maintain bases in Antarctica (see page 9). The scientists and others who live in these are cocooned from the weather in modern facilities, but nonetheless risk being cut off from civilization for long periods. When conditions allow they also leave the stations to go on field trips.

Modern times: a Nunavut hunter in a traditional *parka* uses a satellite phone.

FACT FILE

ALASKA PERMANENT FUND
The Alaska Permanent Fund (APF) is a savings account that belongs to all the people in Alaska. The money in it comes from taxes on mineral developments, including oil.
• Alaska's mineral resources brought the state so much income that in 1980 it abolished individual income tax.
• Each year 50 per cent of the earnings of the APF are divided equally among Alaska's residents.

These houses are in the Inuit territory of Nunavut, Canada. The territory occupies a large part of the Canadian Arctic.

NATIVE PEOPLES

In the Arctic, native peoples such as the Inuit still live in the territories they have occupied for hundreds of years. Their way of life has changed: very few still live on the land as their ancestors did. Instead of tents in summer and dug-in houses in winter, they live in prefabricated homes. These are shipped in ready-made from further south, and assembled into larger communities than used to be the case. Hunters are likely to go out on to the ice using a snowmobile and wearing cold-weather gear filled with down (see page 35), rather than a dog sled and sealskin *parka*.

The change from traditional lifestyles has bought problems for some native people. In particular, alcoholism has affected many communities. On the other hand, they now have access to healthcare and education opportunities that didn't exist in the past.

OIL AND INDUSTRY

Relative new arrivals in the Arctic have been brought there by modern industry. Alaska and Siberia, for example, are both crossed by pipelines hundreds of kilometres long. These were built to carry oil from the oil wells of the far north to distribution centres further to the south. People from the south are drawn to the Arctic lands to work on these and other modern industrial developments.

LOCATION FILE

NUNAVUT

Nunavut (shaded deep blue on the map below) is the name of a region of northern Canada that is now a homeland for Inuit people. They are able to exercise **self-government** there, while remaining part of the Canadian nation.

• Nunavut came into being in 1999; its capital is Iqaluit.

• It covers almost 2,000,000 km², and makes up roughly one-fifth of Canada's area.

• Nunavut means 'Our Land' in an Inuit language.

SUB-ARCTIC PEOPLES

A round the European and Asian fringes of the Arctic live peoples who herd reindeer or caribou. The herds move north in summer. Then in winter they head back south, where the animals spend the cold months in warmer conditions. On the North American fringes of the Arctic, small bands of Native Americans lived by hunting and gathering food. Everywhere these people have seen their traditional ways of life disappearing.

A HERDING EXISTENCE

Groups like the Nenets from Siberia and the Saami from northern Europe traditionally lived by herding reindeer. In winter they headed north to allow the reindeer to **graze** on the mosses and lichens that had been uncovered in the thaw. As the weather turned wintry again, they would pack up their camps and head south, to find warmer pastures.

Twice each year, the reindeer herders of the sub-Arctic make the long journey with their herds to reach new pastures.

FACT FILE

THREATS TO SUB-ARCTIC PEOPLES

There are several key threats to the traditional lifestyles of sub-Arctic peoples:
• Pollution from the former USSR has poisoned the reindeer meat, making it dangerous to eat in some regions.
• Animal rights campaigners have made it impossible to sell the furs of the animals the people hunt or herd.
• Commercial activities, such as logging, oil and gas extraction or hydroelectric power schemes, have made land impossible to use.

AN EXTRACT FROM THE WORK OF YEREMI AIPIN, A KHANT WRITER FROM SIBERIA

The loggers even cut down the trees on the tribal cemetery, thus ruining the final resting place. In all his 76 years, my father had not once plucked a fir needle or a leaf, not a blade of grass unnecessarily on his land, the land of his ancestors.

'What do you want, old man?' I ask my father. 'Can I help you?'

'I don't want anything,' he says after a long silence. 'Only my land. Give me back my land where I can graze my reindeer, hunt game and catch fish. Give me my land where my deer are not attacked by stray dogs and poachers, where the rivers and lakes have no oil slicks – just a patch of my own land.' What can I say in reply?

Below **A village in Chukotka, Siberia. Native peoples in this region found life very difficult under Russia's old communist government, and many still struggle to live their traditional lifestyle.**

CHANGING LIFESTYLES

Today few sub-Arctic peoples live a traditional lifestyle. Only about 10 per cent of Saami people, for example, are still **nomadic** reindeer herders. Most no longer live as they once did. Often their land has been taken for other uses, or ruined by pollution. This loss of their lifestyle, often without anything to replace it, has a bad effect on people. Some fall into despair, and become dependent on alcohol or drugs.

NON-NATIVE PEOPLES

More non-native people also live on the fringes of the Arctic than further north. Oil workers, forestry workers, fishermen, educators and public officials all live in the established communities.

SURVIVAL SKILLS

Life in the polar regions has always been a struggle against the harsh environment. The people of the Arctic developed their clothes and homes in response to the conditions, and usually live safely. But sometimes things go wrong. A hunter may be trapped on the ice by a sudden storm, or become lost in unfamiliar territory. In these situations specialist skills are needed to survive.

SHELTER

Shelter is crucial to anyone caught out in a frozen environment, especially at night. There are various types of snow shelter: the favourite of Inuit people is the *iglu*. Some people think these are what Inuit used to live in, but they have really only ever used them as they do now, for temporary overnight shelter. One alternative is used by Nenets reindeer herders, for example, who carry a tent and stove with them as overnight shelter. A third shelter option is to make a snow cave in a snowy slope.

KEEPING WARM

Unless you have some way of starting a fire, keeping warm in the polar regions in an emergency will probably depend on shelter and clothing. Once you have a shelter arranged, there are a few important ways to help yourself survive. You need to keep your **extremities**, especially your head, warm, as a lot of body heat is lost through them. Unless you're alone, you should cuddle up to the other person or people – even if you don't normally get on with them! You will each lose less body heat this way. You should also wear all your clothes: don't wait to get cold before adding another layer. And you should try not to lie on the ground or snow – a backpack, leaves, branches, almost anything will insulate you from the cold ground, even if only a little.

FACT FILE

SURVIVAL KIT

A polar survival kit could include the following:
• Ice saw, for cutting blocks of ice to make shelter.
• Compass, to avoid walking in circles in the snowy wastes.
• Waterproof matches.
• Plastic survival bag, to crawl inside and retain heat/keep dry.
• Mini solid-fuel stove with fuel.
• Flares.

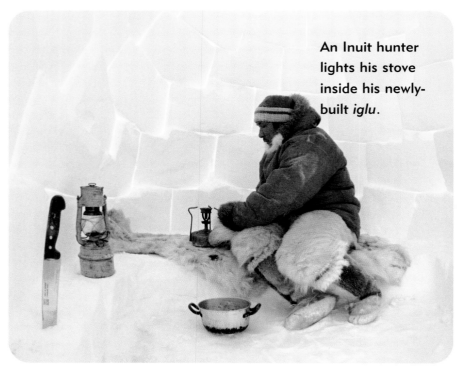

An Inuit hunter lights his stove inside his newly-built *iglu*.

Field training for Antarctic researchers, teaching them how to deal with one of the deadliest environments on Earth.

FACT FILE

RULES FOR AN EMERGENCY SHELTER IN VERY COLD CLIMATES

• If the entrance is lower than the living space, it won't let heat out.

• Make sure the entrance faces away from the wind.

• Ventilate the space with two air holes to avoid suffocation.

• Small shelters are easier to keep warm.

• Keep a digging tool inside, so you can dig yourself out if snowed in.

• Mark the shelter with a flag – it will make the shelter easier to find in the snow.

Top (interior view) and middle (exterior view) **For short stays only – a simple dug-out shelter with an ice-block roof and a brushwood floor for insulation.**

Bottom **A longer-stay shelter – to trap heat this has a low-down door, brushwood insulation and a brushwood cover.**

Ventilation pipes

Brushwood

Ice block roof

Entrance

Sitting area

Sleeping area

Brushwood cover

Ventilation pipe

Sleeping area at a higher level where air is warmer

Low-level ice-block door

POLAR LAND ANIMALS

Penguins and seals visit the coastal areas of Antarctica at times during the year, but no large land-based creatures can survive the climate permanently. The Arctic is a richer environment: because it touches on the surrounding lands, animals have the opportunity to escape the most severe weather.

SPECIAL ADAPTATIONS

Animals that live in the polar regions have to be specially adapted to the extreme conditions. In particular, they need a thick coat to help them survive the icy winds and low temperatures. Arctic hares and foxes have short ears and tails, to stop them losing too much body heat. In the worst of the cold weather, polar animals have a choice: they can either hide from the weather, or travel to warmer lands to escape it.

HIBERNATING FOR WINTER

One way to escape the winter storms and cold is to go to sleep until spring, living off the fat your body has stored during summer. Polar bears, for example, go into a kind of **hibernation** in a cave

Caribou like this one, as well as reindeer, live throughout much of the sub-Arctic. They provide native peoples with meat and skins to make into clothing.

POLAR BEARS
• There are an estimated 25,000 polar bears in the Arctic. About 15,000 of them live in Canada.
• In 1973, Greenland, Norway, Canada, the USA and USSR signed the International Agreement for the Conservation of Polar Bears, in an effort to protect the bears from extinction.
• Nonetheless, polar bears are still threatened by pollution, poaching, hunting, and a shorter hunting season caused by the early springtime melting of the ice in Hudson Bay.

One of the Arctic's most recognizable animals - a polar bear, with her cub.

or snowhole for the winter, before emerging feeling very hungry in the springtime. Polar bear cubs are usually born just before their mother emerges from her hibernation place, so the first weather they see is the Arctic spring.

ESCAPING THE COLD
Some animals head south of the true Arctic for the winter. Herds of caribou and reindeer, for example, spend the warmer summer months grazing on the tundra. During the winter, as the temperatures on the tundra get colder, they head south. The winter can be spent in the shelter of the evergreen taiga forests, where the temperatures are higher and there is more protection from the wind.

FACT FILE

AN ANTARCTIC GIANT
The largest land animal in Antarctica is an insect less than 1.3 cm long. It is a wingless midge (if it had wings the wind would blow it away) that hops on its tail to get around, and usually lives near penguin colonies.

POLAR SEA CREATURES

During the feeding season in Antarctica, a full-grown blue whale eats about 40 million krill (shrimp-like creatures) a day. That's enough to feed a human for four years! Yet the seas are so rich that there are enough krill to support this feeding.

PLANKTON

One of the most important parts of the polar ocean **food chain** is plankton, tiny creatures that thrive in the polar seas. Plantlike organisms among the plankton are called phytoplankton, while the animal organisms are called zooplankton. Krill, for example, are a type of zooplankton.

The plankton is eaten by other sea creatures, from small fish (which are then eaten by bigger fish) to the world's largest animal, the blue whale.

The male Atlantic walrus can grow to almost 4 m long and weigh 1,400 kg. Its tusks can reach 1 m in length.

AQUATIC ANIMALS

Animals like whales, dolphins and fish are fully aquatic – they spend all their time in the sea. In the past these animals have provided a rich resource. Cod in particular has been a popular catch around the Arctic for hundreds of years. There is even evidence that Basque cod fishermen reached North America long before Columbus – but kept it secret because of the rich cod-fishing grounds off the coast! In Antarctica the main commercial fish is the Patagonian toothfish.

AMPHIBIOUS ANIMALS

Some animals – penguins, seals and walruses, for example – hunt for food in the sea but rest on land. This 'wet n' dry' lifestyle is called amphibious. The amphibious animals eat fish and shellfish, and are in turn hunted by one of the world's most fearsome predators, the killer whale.

THE GRAND BANKS

The Grand Banks is a fishing ground off the coast of Newfoundland. Plankton thrive in the shallow waters, which attracts fish, including cod, in large numbers. The cod provide a good example of what can happen when a polar resource is overused.

Today the cod have been **over-fished**. The fish caught in the north Atlantic are far smaller than those of two hundred years ago, which were the size of a fully-grown man. Cod numbers have probably reached a point where they cannot recover (see pages 36–37).

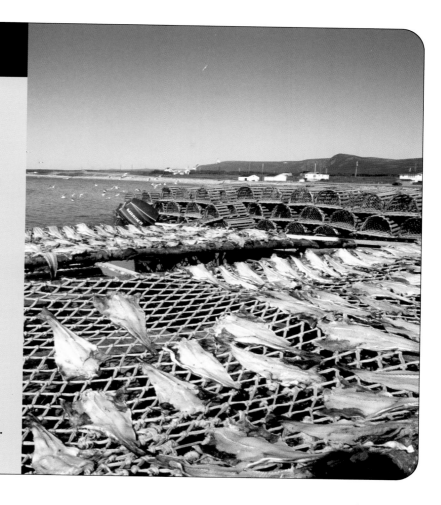

Cod drying in the Newfoundland sun.

POLAR BIRDS
- The old squaw duck, willow ptarmigans and eider ducks are the most common Arctic birds.
- The eider duck's soft breast feathers are especially prized for use in duvets, sleeping bags and warm coats, as they trap air for warmth but are extremely light.
- Penguins (left) are the Antarctic's most common birds. Their coat of feathers is waterproof and they have a thick layer of fat for insulation against the cold.

A colony of penguins in Antarctica.

COMMERCIAL EXPLOITATIO

T he polar regions are unique environments that have built up over hundreds of thousands of years. They can easily be changed by pollution, mineral extraction, farming of their natural resources (such as seals or whales) and settlement by humans. Once they are damaged it is uncertain when, or even whether, they would recover.

WHALING AND FISHING

Fishing and whaling provide good examples of how the polar environment can be changed by human actions. During the eighteenth and nineteenth centuries, the world's whales were hunted by large fleets of ships. Some species were brought to the brink of extinction.

During the twentieth century cod was fished to such high levels that it seems unlikely ever to recover. Breeding stocks are now so low that the cod may have lost their place on the food chain. They would find it impossible to increase their numbers, because their food resources are being eaten by other species.

This gas-drilling rig is in Siberia. Oil and gas are among the Arctic's richest resources.

THE ARCTIC NATIONAL WILDLIFE RESERVE

In 2002 this reserve in north-eastern Alaska was threatened with being opened to oil drilling.

• President Bush claimed that the reserve could be part of a long-term answer to the USA's 'energy crisis'.

• Opponents said that the drilling and pipelines would have a serious effect on the wildlife within the reserve, especially caribou (below) and muskoxen, whose migration routes would be interrupted.

• The US Geological Survey had said in 1998 that only 3.2–5.2 billion barrels of oil were recoverable from the reserve – a six-month supply for the USA.

On 18 April 2002 the US Senate voted against allowing oilmen into the reserve.

Below **Caribou swim large distances on their migration routes. Their overland migration routes would be cut if oil drilling starts in the Arctic National Wildlife Reserve.**

ARCTIC COMMERCIAL ACTIVITY

In the Arctic, big businesses are keen to make money by extracting the region's minerals. There is already oil drilling, gas extraction and mining in the Arctic. Even places that are supposed to be protected, such as wildlife reserves, are sometimes not safe.

THE ANTARCTIC TREATY

The Antarctic is run through the Antarctic Treaty, which was signed by 12 countries in 1961. Since then 32 other countries have joined, and the Treaty represents 80 per cent of the world's people. It says that the Antarctic is a natural reserve, devoted to peace and scientific research.

POLLUTION

With little industry of their own and a very low population density, you might think that the polar regions would not suffer from pollution. In fact, pollution reaches polar seas on ocean currents, and polar lands through the air. This is especially true of the Arctic, which lies nearer to major industrial nations.

OIL POLLUTION

In both Alaska and Siberia, long oil pipelines carry oil from the oilfields to ice-free tanker ports. Leaks in the pipelines can spread crude oil over a large area very quickly. This affects the animals and people who live there, and can **contaminate** the soil for many years.

Oil also pollutes the seas and coasts of the polar regions. In 1989 the oil tanker *Exxon Valdez* ran aground in Prince William Sound in Alaska. The tanker spilled nearly 50 million litres of oil, which was still affecting local wildlife years later.

RADIOACTIVITY

In Siberia reindeer pastures have been affected by fallout (radioactive pollution) from nuclear testing done during the Cold War (see page 7). Then in 1986, an accident at the Chernobyl nuclear power plant in Ukraine spread radioactive pollution right across northern Europe and into the Arctic. The reindeer pastures were contaminated, making it impossible for many herders to sell reindeer meat. Some were forced away from their traditional lifestyles.

Part of the huge clean-up operation after the Exxon Valdez oil spill in 1989.

POLLUTION AND THE FOOD CHAIN

Once some pollutants (**organochlorines**, for example) reach the polar regions in the air or on ocean currents, they **concentrate** on their way up the food chain. For example, imagine 100 small fish have 0.01 g of pollutant inside them. These are eaten by a larger fish, which then has 1 g of pollutant. Then a seal eats 100 of the larger fish, meaning it has 100 g of pollutant. If a polar bear manages to eat several seals, it will quickly develop very high levels of pollutants.

Some other, more toxic pollutants (such as **organophosphates**) do not concentrate in the same way.

FACT FILE

POLLUTED POLAR BEARS

• On Norway's Svalbard Islands scientists are worried that levels of PCBs among polar bears are far higher than in North America. Norwegian polar bears have PCB levels that can be over 2.5 times as high as their American cousins.
• In parts of Canada PCB levels among polar bears are also excessive.
• In Russia the polar bear population is said to have PCB levels 17 times as high as in North America.

PEOPLE FILE

THE SAAMI

The Saami live in northern Norway, Sweden, Finland and Russia.
• In 1986, the Chernobyl nuclear disaster spread radioactive pollution across Saami pastures. Unable to sell or eat their reindeer meat, many Saami left their traditional way of life.
• Even worse, it emerged later that the level of contamination was very low and probably the ban was a panic reaction, which did more harm than good. Selling reindeer meat from the pastures was banned.

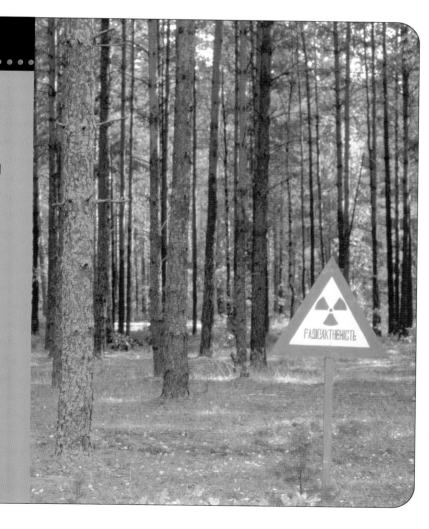

Signs warn that this forest near Chernobyl, Ukraine is dangerous because of radioactivity.

GLOBAL WARMING

The Antarctic ice cap is the largest body of fresh water in the world, about 70 per cent of the world's total. If this ice were to melt, sea levels would rise. The effects of this could be catastrophic. Fortunately this is not predicted to happen for thousands of years, if ever: the world's temperature is rising worldwide by about 1.7 °C per century.

Environmental campaigners say that the reason for temperature rises is that the world produces too many greenhouse gases, especially carbon dioxide. These gases help trap heat in the atmosphere, leading to a rise in temperature known as global warming (see diagram right).

SEA LEVEL RISES

The Antarctic ice cap alone contains enough water to raise sea levels by 60–65 m. Environmentalists fear that if sea levels rose by even a fraction of this it would cause huge problems. Major cities such as New York and Los Angeles would be threatened by flooding. Coastal plains, where food is often grown, would be underwater. The world's growing population would be squeezed into an ever-smaller space.

TEMPERATURE RISE AND THE ICE CAPS

In fact, so far the rises in temperature seem to be having little effect on the ice caps. The West Antarctic Ice Sheet has been losing mass for several thousand years – since long before concerns about global temperature rises – and the rate of loss remains constant. The East Antarctic Ice Sheet is stable and likely to remain so: melting it would require a temperature rise of more than 20 °C. The Greenland Ice Sheet is losing mass in some places, but the effect is minimal.

The Greenhouse Effect: the name given to the process where too much of the Sun's heat is trapped in the Earth's atmosphere, leading to global warming. Heat from the Sun warms the atmosphere and the land (1). Some heat escapes (2), but more heat is absorbed by the atmosphere (3), adding to the overall temperature.

FACT FILE

RISES IN SEA LEVEL

• Arctic sea ice has thinned by 40 per cent in the past three decades, and its extent has possibly shrunk by as much as 10 to 15 per cent.

• The global average sea level has risen by 10 to 20 cm over the past 100 years. It is expected to rise by another 11 to 77 cm by 2100.

CHANGES IN TEMPERATURE

Scientists have examined cores of ice from Greenland and Antarctica to discover whether changes in carbon dioxide levels cause temperature changes:

• The ancient ice provides a record of the atmosphere for the past 160,000 years. During those years, the climate warmed and cooled several times.

• Researchers analyzed the gases that were trapped in the ice when it formed.

• During cooler periods, the atmosphere contained about 30 per cent less carbon dioxide than in warmer periods. (It is likely that the change in carbon dioxide concentration was a consequence of climate change, not its cause. The carbon dioxide level rose some centuries after the temperature rose.)

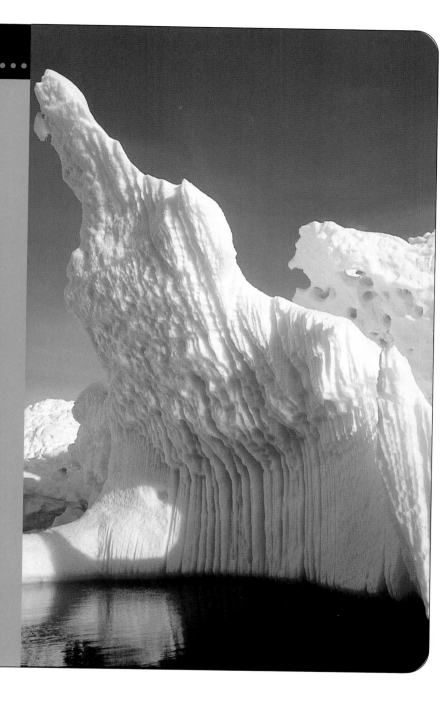

Warmer air has caused this ice in Antarctica to melt into a layered pattern. The honeycombing in the ice in the background is also caused by temperature rise.

THE KYOTO PROTOCOL

In 1997, 38 of the world's nations agreed in the Kyoto Protocol to try to cut their greenhouse gas emissions. Unfortunately they have been largely unsuccessful. The USA, the world's biggest polluter, has backed out of the Protocol, and other nations are lukewarm about supporting it. The main factor is the economic cost. Governments also worry that their populations, used to car ownership and other luxuries of modern life, will react badly to having some of these reduced.

In the light of this, sea levels seem likely to rise over the coming decades. The most recent estimate is for a rise of 0.11–0.77 m (best estimate 0.49 m) between 1990 and 2100. This is unlikely to have drastic global consequences, but could have a serious effect on some low-lying coastal regions.

POLAR TOURISM

Despite their inhospitable nature, the polar regions are attracting increasing numbers of tourists. People come to see the wildlife, experience the unique environment, see the **Northern** or **Southern Lights,** or to go hunting. Antarctica is even home to a very small mountaineering industry!

LIFESTYLE TOURISM

Some people come to the polar lands, usually the Arctic, to get a taste of the lifestyle of its native peoples. They can ride a dog sled, be guided on the ice by Inuit guides, go **ice-hole fishing** – even learn to build an *iglu*. These tourists tend to bring money to the local economy, because local people provide them with a service for which they are paid.

WILDLIFE TOURS

Other tourists come to see the polar wildlife. For example, in Churchill, Canada, it's possible to see polar bears out on the ice. Some bears even wander into town, where they can be watched from the safety of a taxi or from indoors! Other polar settlements specialize in whale-watching visits or trips to see sea lions. Again, this type of tourism brings money to the local economy.

CRUISING

Cruising – being transported from place to place on a **self-contained** luxury boat – is increasingly popular in polar waters. Passengers get to see icebergs and the ice shelf up close, as well as the animals that live there. They suffer little of the discomfort associated with the polar seas, as they can stay warm in their cabins and eat food like that found in any hotel around the world.

An Inuit park warden on Ellesmere Island, Canada, shows tourists how an old stone fox trap worked.

These tourists in the Antarctic have abandoned their ship for smaller boats, so that they can get a closer look at a seal.

 FACT FILE

TEN PRINCIPLES FOR ARCTIC TOURISM

These ground rules come from WWF, the global environment network:

1 Make tourism and conservation compatible.
2 Support the preservation of wilderness and **biodiversity**.
3 Use natural resources in a sustainable way.
4 Minimise consumption, waste and pollution.
5 Respect local cultures.
6 Respect historic and scientific sites.
7 Arctic communities should benefit from tourism.
8 Trained staff are the key to responsible tourism.
9 Make your trip an opportunity to learn about the Arctic.
10 Follow safety rules.

A tourist photographs a penguin chick in Antarctica.

FUTURE CHALLENGES

The polar regions are a unique **biome** (a region of the Earth with a characteristic climate and type of vegetation). The living things that can survive in them have adapted to an environment different from almost anywhere else on Earth. If the Arctic or Antarctic regions change significantly, many of the creatures that live in them will die out. They are not adapted to life in any other place.

Oil spills from a pipeline in Siberia. Oil leaks such as this are damaging the Arctic environment.

ENVIRONMENTAL CHALLENGES

Pollution, from oil and gas drilling as well as from outside the polar regions, is a major challenge for the future. The nations that fringe the Arctic now have cleaner industries than was the case 50 years ago. For example, PCBs are no longer widely used in industrial processes, and were banned entirely in the USA in 1979. However, radioactive contamination and oil spills continue to affect the Arctic.

FACT FILE

POLLUTION LEVELS

A 2002 study commissioned by the US Senate Environment and Public Works Committee assessed likely increases in pollution levels from fossil fuels:

• Electricity generation in the USA was forecast to increase 42 per cent by 2020.

• Annual carbon dioxide emissions from power plants will rise nationwide by about 725 million tonnes.

• Emissions of carbon dioxide will increase in all areas of the USA, with a total increase of 3 per cent.

Global warming is the major environmental challenge for both polar regions. No one is sure of the exact effect global warming will have on the polar ice, but there are already signs of it melting in unexpected places. If this continues it will pose a global problem, with whole low-lying countries such as Bangladesh being drowned.

The difficulty is that the causes of global warming lie outside the Arctic, in the world's big industrial processes. Unless the world community decides to act together to halt temperature rises, progress is likely to be slow and inadequate.

HUMAN ISSUES

Another challenge for the Arctic is the culture of its people. It is becoming increasingly hard for native people to maintain anything like a traditional lifestyle. Only about 10 per cent of Saami people still follow a traditional herding lifestyle, for example. In Canada, Inuit people find it hard to keep up elements of their traditional hunting lifestyle: they cannot sell the furs of the animals they hunt, because of a worldwide ban on seal-fur sales. On the positive side, Inuit people are able to have a far bigger say in governing their own affairs since the creation of their Nunavut homeland.

FACT FILE

THE ANTARCTIC

Global warming aside, the Antarctic faces fewer challenges than the Arctic:
• The Antarctic Treaty protects it from territorial disputes or commercial exploitation.
• The Antarctic is further from regions with high human populations, as well as being far from major industrial centres, so it receives less pollution from outside.

Below **Penguins dwarfed by a giant glacier.**

GLOSSARY

Baleen Also known as whalebone, baleen comprises sheets of horn-like material, the lower part fringed with bristles, that hang from the roof of the mouth of filter-feeding whales. It is used to strain plankton out of sea water. Whalebone formerly had several uses, including as stays in women's corsets.

Banishment Being sent away from your community to live elsewhere.

Biodiversity A wide range of different living things, adapted to a range of different environments.

Biome A region of the Earth with a characteristic climate and type of vegetation, such as desert, tropical forest, or polar ice.

Cold War A state of tension between the two most powerful countries on Earth, the USA and the USSR. The Cold War began in the late 1940s and began to end in the late 1980s. The USSR broke apart in 1991, finally ending its rivalry with the USA.

Concentrate To make stronger, usually by bringing together more of a particular thing. For example, an army might concentrate its forces on an enemy position by bringing more soldiers to fight in that particular place.

Contaminate To make impure or pollute.

Density The mass, or weight, of a substance in relation to its volume. Lead is denser than wood, for example, because a given volume of lead is heavier than the same volume of wood.

Extremities The fingers, hands, arms, toes, feet, legs and head; the ends of the parts of the human body that are attached to the torso.

Food chain A group of interrelated living things that depend on one another for food, by eating one another. For example, plankton are eaten by fish, which are in turn eaten by seals and seals are eaten by killer whales.

Fresh water Water from rain, which is not salty like sea water.

Graze To feed on growing grass or herbs.

Hibernation Spending winter in a state of deep sleep.

Icebreakers Ships that are specially equipped to break a path through icy seas.

Ice-hole fishing Catching fish by dangling a line through a hole cut in the sea ice.

Iglu A temporary shelter made of blocks of ice and snow, used by Inuit hunters as temporary accommodation.

Income tax A tax (payment to the government) paid as a proportion of what someone earns.

Katabatic wind The movement of cold, dense air down a slope.

Kayak A long narrow boat with a covered deck, paddled using a single oar that has a blade on each end.

Meltwater Water produced by melted snow or ice.

Migratory Moving from one place to another, usually in search of food.

Nomadic Living in different places at different times of the year, usually to make sure that herd animals have food. Nenets reindeer herders, for example, spend winter in the taiga forests and summer on the tundra.

Northern lights Streams and bands of light that appear in the night sky near the Arctic Circle. Also known as the aurora borealis.

North-west Passage A route from Europe to Asia across or around northern North America. From 1524 to 1906, when Roald Amundsen completed the first voyage through the passage, navigators searched for such a route.

Organochlorine A kind of long-lasting pesticide containing chlorine atoms, which is used to control insects, normally to stop them affecting crops.

Organophosphates A kind of pesticide containing phosphorus atoms, which is not harmful to crops but can be extremely harmful to people and animals.

Over-fished When numbers of fish are reduced by so many that they are unlikely to recover.

PCBs (polychlorinated biphenyls) Chemicals that were once commonly used in industrial processes. Studies later showed that exposure to PCBs can cause birth defects, cancer, liver disorders and nerve damage.

Permafrost The layer of soil in polar regions that remains frozen throughout the year.

Photosynthesis The process by which plants manufacture sugars using light for energy.

Plateau A high, flat area of land.

Precipitation Rain, snow, sleet, fog, frost, dew, ice or hail.

Self-contained Independent; not needing to take help or supplies from elsewhere.

Self-government A limited form of independence, where an area within a bigger country is given the right to make its own decisions about certain aspects of life.

Southern lights Streams and bands of light that appear in the night sky near the Antarctic Circle. Also known as the aurora australis.

Spermaceti A waxy material in the heads of sperm whales and bottlenose whales, which can be used to make candles. It is also used in some face creams, and as a lubricant.

Sub-Arctic Regions south of the Arctic where the summer temperature rises over 10 °C (50 °F), though not for more than four months of the year.

Umiak A traditional Inuit boat covered mainly with skins. Umiaks are larger and wider than kayaks.

USSR Union of Soviet Socialist Republics, the country that from 1917 to 1991 controlled large areas of territory in Russia, eastern Europe, and northern and western Asia.

Walrus ivory Material from the tusks of male walrus.

Whale oil Oil taken from the blubber (rubbery flesh) of whales.

Wind chill A description of the effect the wind has on temperature. For example, a strong wind can make a warm day feel chilly, because it whips the heat away from your body.

WEBSITES TO VISIT

www.antarctica.ac.uk
This is the site of the British Antarctic Survey. Full of information, and it's even possible to get in contact with someone living in one of the Antarctic research stations.
British Antarctic Survey
High Cross, Madingley Road
Cambridge CB3 0ET, UK
Tel: 01223 221400
Email: information@bas.ac.uk

www.spri.cam.ac.uk
The site of the Scott Polar Research Institute: not only a mine of useful information, but also a good place to find a very extensive links section to other polar sites.
Scott Polar Research Institute
University of Cambridge, Lensfield Road
Cambridge CB2 1ER, UK
Tel: 01223 336540
Email: enquiries@spri.cam.ac.uk

www.mnh.si.edu/arctic
Site for the Smithsonian Institution's Arctic Studies Center, which focuses on the lives and history of northern peoples.
Arctic Studies Center
Department of Anthropology
National Museum of Natural History
Smithsonian Institution
Washington, DC 20560-0112, USA
Tel +1 202-357-2682
Email: arctics@nmnh.si.edu

BOOKS TO READ

Polar Animals by Michael Chinery (Kingfisher Books, 1995)

True Polar Adventure Stories by Paul Dowswell (Usborne Publishing Ltd, 2002)

Saving Our World: *Polar Regions* by Jen Green (Franklin Watts, 2003)

Arctic and Antarctic by Barbara Taylor, Geoff Brightling (photographer) (DK Eyewitness Books, 2000)

INDEX